Understanding
Grace Giving

Mark H. Ballard

NORTHEASTERN BAPTIST PRESS

Bennington, Vermont

To Cindy and Ben

PREFACE

Over a two-year period of time Pastor Mark Ballard led Christian Fellowship Baptist Church on a Journey Through the Bible. Each week the Sunday Morning, Sunday Night and Wednesday Night services were dedicated to a single book of Scripture. As the Church came to 2 Corinthians Pastor Mark sensed the Lord leading him to spend three weeks on this book. During that three-week period of time he preached 3 sermons on the subject of *Grace Giving*. These three sermons served as background preparation for the development of this booklet.

Very few subjects raise emotions like the subject of giving. Some pastors avoid the subject altogether. Others seem to overemphasize it so much that people feel that all the church ever does is ask for money. Even among those who preach and teach on giving there seems to be tension. Some emphasize *tithing* as the essential standard. Others emphasize *Grace Giving* as the priority concept in giving. Some simply advise their listeners to give whatever they desire, or to not give at all.

In this short booklet Pastor Mark explains his own journey in dealing with the subject of giving. He describes his own struggle with knowing how to deal with the Biblical concepts in a time when many television preachers were abusing the subject. He then shares how the Lord moved in his heart to settle the issue once and for all. In addition to explaining his own journey, Pastor Mark leads the reader through an examination of three critical texts of Scripture that teach the meaning of *Grace Giving*.

The Top Ten List

Imagine if you were asked to participate in a survey of church members across America. The survey asked one simple question. List the top 10 topics on which you like to hear your pastor preach. What would be on your list?

If this survey were done it is highly unlikely that *Grace Giving* would make the final cut. In fact, many faithful church attendees would rather avoid the Sundays the pastor addresses giving. To be honest, many pastors would also like to avoid those Sundays. During our first church plant I must admit that *money* and *giving* were topics I did my best to avoid.

We started our first church during a time when many TV preachers were abusing the subject of giving. They would promise great rewards for those who gave. The TV viewers would give and give and give only to find out that the entire "ministry" had turned into an elaborate scam. I remember one particular television preacher that used his airtime to play on the sympathies of his audience. He was shown walking through a burnt-out house and talking about the fire he and his wife suffered. The scene clearly touched the hearts of the viewers. Money poured into the pastor's office. Within a short time, it was learned that the house pictured on the program was one of many homes owned by the preacher. In fact, it was not even his primary residence.

Starting a church in this type of environment caused me to be extremely cautious about the subject of *giving*. I went to an extreme in the opposite direction. I decided that we would not make giving a part of our worship service at all. Instead, we placed a small basket on a table at the back of the room. Every Sunday I would put my offering in the basket and simply hope that people would understand that for the church to survive they needed to give. On rare occasions I would mention the basket was there for those who felt led to help with the needs of the church.

Though we saw many people come to faith and follow the Lord in believer's baptism, the church never became a self-supporting congregation. This taught me a little about the importance of giving to the survival of the church. However, the Lord used His Word to radically alter my view on giving. He did this through several passages of Scripture, but the largest impact came from Paul's relationship to the Corinthian church.

In 2 Corinthians chapters eleven and twelve Paul speaks of his relationship to the Church at Corinth. In doing so he discusses the fact that he preached to them "free of charge",[1] indicating that he did not receive financial support from them. He then tells them that he "robbed other churches, taking wages from them to minister to you (the Corinthians).[2] However, the most striking statement

---

1   2 Corinthians 11:7
2   2 Corinthians 11:8

comes when Paul asks the Corinthians to forgive him for wronging them by refusing to accept financial support.[3]

Of all the difficult issues Paul had to address in the Corinthian church, this is the only place where he asked them to forgive him. They had not learned to support those who preached the Gospel. They had not learned to worship the Lord through the ministry of *Grace Giving*. The day the Lord brought this home to me I had to repent. I sought the Lord's forgiveness for not teaching the new believers in that first church plant the importance of *Grace Giving*. I then asked the Lord to help me to never avoid teaching Biblical truths again. Therefore, it is in the spirit of obedience to the Lord and His Word that I offer this booklet. Let's learn together of the importance of *Grace Giving*.

THE FOCUS

The Tithe

Once we understand that giving is important the question comes, "what should be our focus?" Some would argue that when we speak of *giving* our focus should be on the *tithe*. The word *tithe* means *a tenth* and generally conveys the idea that 10% of all we own belongs to the Lord. The *tithe* was the focus of giving throughout the Old Testa-

---

3   2 Corinthians 12:13

ment. It was expected that everyone would give a *tithe* of all they owned. In fact, we see numerous occasions in the Old Testament where God's hand of blessing was withheld because of the lack of tithing. We also can find several occasions where the Lord judged His people for avoiding the tithe. The prophet Malachi explained that when the people of God withheld the tithe they were "robbing God."[4]

Grace Giving

Others would argue that *tithing* was an Old Testament concept designed for the Children of Israel. These would further indicate that the concept of *tithing* is not found in the New Testament. Since we are "not under the law"[5], we are not bound by the *tithe*. Many who take this position refer to *Grace Giving* as the New Testament concept. The basic idea is that we live under grace and should give out of a heart of gratitude to the Lord not by compulsion.[6]

Coming Into Focus

Is *tithing* an Old Testament concept? Yes! Is *Grace Giving* a New Testament concept? Yes! Are both the Old and New Testaments God's Word? Absolutely! Therefore, we

---

4   Malachi 3:8–10

5   Galatians 5:18

6   2 Corinthians 9:7

must learn from both concepts. Remember, Jesus said that He did not come to destroy the Law but to fulfill it.[7] The fact is Jesus fulfilled the law on our behalf. Receiving His free gift of grace empowers us to live out the realities of righteousness as He lives His life through us.[8] Of course, we must understand that when Jesus lives His life through us, we go beyond the letter of the law and fulfill the spirit of the law. Consider Jesus' words:

> Do not think that I came to destroy the Law or the Prophets. I did not come to destroy but to fulfill. "For assuredly, I say to you, till heaven and earth pass away, one jot or one tittle will by no means pass from the law till all is fulfilled. "Whoever therefore breaks one of the least of these commandments, and teaches men so, shall be called least in the kingdom of heaven; but whoever does and teaches them, he shall be called great in the kingdom of heaven. "For I say to you, that unless your righteousness exceeds the righteousness of the scribes and Pharisees, you will by no means enter the kingdom of heaven. "You have heard that it was said to those of old, 'You shall not murder, and whoever murders will be in danger of the judgment.' "But I say to you that whoever

---

7   Matthew 5:17
8   Galatians 2:20

is angry with his brother without a cause shall be in danger of the judgment. And whoever says to his brother, 'Raca!' shall be in danger of the council. But whoever says, 'You fool!' shall be in danger of hell fire. "Therefore if you bring your gift to the altar, and there remember that your brother has something against you, "leave your gift there before the altar, and go your way. First be reconciled to your brother, and then come and offer your gift. "Agree with your adversary quickly, while you are on the way with him, lest your adversary deliver you to the judge, the judge hand you over to the officer, and you be thrown into prison. "Assuredly, I say to you, you will by no means get out of there till you have paid the last penny. "You have heard that it was said to those of old, 'You shall not commit adultery.' "But I say to you that whoever looks at a woman to lust for her has already committed adultery with her in his heart.[9]

There are several key concepts that can be observed in the New Testament about living under *Grace*. First, it is not about what I do but about what Jesus did for me.[10] Thus, we are saved by Christ's work not our own. Second,

---

9   Matthew 5:17–28
10   Ephesians 2:8–9

it is not about what I do as a believer but what Christ does through me.[11] Therefore, we live the Christian life just as we entered the Christian life – "by grace through faith."[12] Third, when Christ lives through us, we will do nothing against the law but will in fact supersede the law.[13]

In light of these truths let me attempt to draw several key conclusions regarding the subject of giving:

1. Giving is a Biblical Concept that is evident in both the Old and New Testaments.
2. The focus in the Old Testament was on the *Tithe*.
3. The Old Testament is God's Word.
4. The focus in the New Testament is on *Grace Giving*.
5. *Grace Giving* is most clearly expressed as Christ lives through us.
6. If Christ came to fulfill the law and if we submit to Him allowing Him to live His Life through us, then we will give.
7. If under the law people were expected to give ten percent of all their increase to the Lord, then it is impossible for someone living under grace to give less than those who lived under the law.

---

11 Galatians 2:20
12 Colossians 2:6
13 Galatians 5:16–26

So what is *Grace Giving* all about? Who should give? When should we give? How much should we give? How do I know if I am really giving as the Lord wants me to give? These questions and more will be answered as we consider the most extensive passage of Scripture on the subject of *Grace Giving*.

In 2 Corinthians chapters eight and nine the Apostle Paul addresses the issues of *Grace Giving*. As you read through this text it becomes obvious that *grace giving* is the theme. Paul writes to the Corinthians about receiving an offering for support of the churches in Judea. Yet in discussing giving, six times in these two chapters the Apostle refers to "the grace of God." It is because of and through the Grace of God that we are to give.

As we consider these two chapters our focus will be on three of the five paragraphs. In the first paragraph we will learn that *Grace Giving* follows **The Example Of The Macedonians** (2 Corinthians 8:1-7). In the second paragraph we will learn that *Grace Giving* follows **The Example Of The Messiah** (2 Corinthians 8:8-15). During our consideration of a third paragraph we will learn that *Grace Giving* follows **The Exhortations Of The Missionary** (2 Corinthians 9:6-15).

The Example of
the Macedonians

Moreover, brethren, we make known to you the grace of God bestowed on the churches of Macedonia: that in a great trial of affliction the abundance of their joy and their deep poverty abounded in the riches of their liberality. For I bear witness that according to their ability, yes, and beyond their ability, they were freely willing, imploring us with much urgency that we would receive the gift and the fellowship of the ministering to the saints. And not only as we had hoped, but they first gave themselves to the Lord, and then to us by the will of God. So we urged Titus, that as he had begun, so he would also complete this grace in you as well. But as you abound in everything—in faith, in speech, in knowledge, in all diligence, and in your love for us—see that you abound in this grace also.[14]

Paul begins his discussion of *Grace Giving* by pointing to the example of the believers living in Macedonia. About a year earlier the Corinthians had promised to give to a special offering providing relief to the saints in Judea. At the time, Paul used their commitment as an example to the Macedonians. They were inspired by Paul's

---

14 2 Corinthians 8:1–7

testimony and really set the standard in giving. Now that a year had passed, the Corinthians had not made good on their promise to give. Thus, Paul writes 2 Corinthians 8:1-7 and encourages the Corinthians to follow the example of the Macedonians who not only promised to give but they made good on their commitment.

The Macedonians set the standard in giving by being an example in four specific ways. First, they gave out of their poverty. Second, they gave beyond their ability. Third, they gave willingly. Fourth, they gave with the right priority. These four principles help us to begin to understand what it means to be involved in *Grace Giving*. Let us take a few minutes to consider each of these principles.

They Gave Out Of Their Poverty

Paul begins explaining the example of the Macedonians by pointing to the Grace of God, which was at work in their lives. Verse one clearly states that God's Grace working in the lives of these early believers is what led them to give. Giving begins in the heart of God Himself. The Greek word *didomi* translated here as *bestowed*, literally means, *to give*. In grace He gave to us His only begotten Son so that we might have life.[15] Furthermore, He gave us all things necessary for life and godliness.[16]

---

15 John 3:16
16 2 Peter 1:1-4

Understanding the giving heart of the Father motivated them to get involved in *Grace Giving*. Because God has given, the Macedonians wanted to give. Because God has given, we too should be motivated to give.

Not only did they give out of the Grace of God, but they also gave out of their own poverty. In verse two Paul testifies that the Macedonians were suffering "a great trial of affliction" and "deep poverty." Yet they set the standard in giving. In Greek we find the words, *bathos ptocheia* to describe their situation. The Macedonians were *down in the depths of poverty*. In other words, they could not afford to give. Yet, they gave out of a heart of gratitude for the grace of God.

Though this is surprising, a bigger surprise comes when you consider two other words found in the verse that are used to describe their giving. Paul says the Macedonians not only gave, but they also gave *liberally*. The Greek word is *haplotes* which means that they gave *with simplicity, bountifully, and selflessly*. If this were not enough, the text says that they gave *liberally* with *chara* or *joy*. In other words, they joyfully gave according to the grace of God, out of their own deep poverty. Wow! What an example!

Elijah, no doubt, understood the amazement that Paul must have felt. When he was in need the Lord sent him not to the palace of a rich man but to the humble cottage of a poor widow who had one meal worth of provisions left. Yet, as she gave out of her poverty, the Lord miraculously met her needs allowing her to provide food for herself, her son, and the prophet of God (1 Kings 17;8-16). Our giving should not be based on how well off we are at the moment.

Our giving should be based on the grace of God. We should give based on what He leads us to give out of a heart of love for Him, even if our giving does not make sense to others. When things get tight financially many individuals begin to cut back on their giving to the Lord and His work. In fact, many churches do the same thing. When the economy is down the first place some churches cut the budget is the missions giving. Yet this approach is just opposite of the example of the Macedonians. The Corinthians made big promises, had big pocketbooks, but gave little. The Macedonians did not boast and had little; but they gave out of their poverty.

They Gave Beyond Their Ability

As we come to verse three Paul specifically states that he bears witness to their giving. The Greek word *martureo* is here used to indicate that he was an eyewitness willing to give testimony to the fact of the sacrificial giving of the Macedonians. He could testify that these believers gave in accordance with their *ability*. Usually translated as *power*, the Greek word, *dunamis* is here translated as *ability*. In other words, they gave all they had the *power* to give.

As if this sacrifice were not enough, Paul says they even went beyond their own *ability* in giving. The Greek word *huper* indicates that they gave *exceedingly abundantly, above and beyond*. He then bears witness to the fact that they were still *freely willing* to give more. What an example the Macedonians set for the Corinthians and for all believers of all times.

Several years ago, my own pastor shared how that the Lord taught him about this kind of sacrificial giving. While in seminary he served as the pastor of a small congregation. One Sunday as he received his weekly paycheck the Lord began to move on his heart to give it back to the church in the offering plate. Of course, Roy knew that he needed gas for his car and food for his family. Yet he sensed the Lord clearly leading him to give the entire check. Following the leading of the Lord, he placed the check in the offering plate, giving sacrificially and willingly. He gave not only according to his ability, but he gave beyond his ability and trusted the Lord to provide gas and food for the week.[17]

The Lord honored Roy's obedient sacrifice and provided for every need he and his family had that week. In fact, by the time the next Sunday arrived, the Lord had provided a full 90% of his weekly check back into his

---

17 Roy Spannagel, Sermon on Luke 6:38 ar First Southern Baptist Church in Pueblo, CO, c. 1984

hands through various unexpected sources.[18] Roy learned when God's people give sacrificially, trusting Him to meet their own needs, He always provides for them.

They Gave Willingly

Look again at the last phrase of verse three. Paul says that the Macedonians gave because they were "freely willing." Here we have the Greek word, *authairetos* indicating that they gave out of their own free will. No one forced them to give. No one manipulated them to give through guilt. No one commanded them to give. They simply gave willingly out of a heart of grace, following the example of our loving Lord.

In verse four we learn that they were so willing that they "implored" Paul to hurry and receive the gift with "urgency." The word translated as *implore* is the Greek *deomai* meaning to *beseech* or *beg*. In our day we can turn on the television and see "preachers" begging for people to send them money. When was the last time you saw someone begging to give money to the Lord's work? That is exactly what the Macedonians did. They were so willing that they begged for the opportunity to give.

They begged to give because they wanted to be a part of the "fellowship of ministering to the saints." The word *fellowship* is often misunderstood today. Many

---

18 Ibid.

times, when we hear people talk of *fellowship* we think of a church eating a meal together. However, that is simply one aspect of the Greek word *koinonia*. Literally the word indicates a *partnership*. The Macedonians could not go with Paul to minister to those in Judea. However, they could become *partners* in this ministry through their giving. And so, they willingly *begged* to participate by giving sacrificially.

We see this kind of free will giving exampled for us in Exodus chapters thirty-five and thirty-six. At the instruction of the Lord, Moses called for the people to give for the building of the Tabernacle. In these chapters we see everyone freely giving to the cause. They had a heart to give so that a beautiful place of worship could be constructed. They gave gold, silver, and precious stones. They gave cloth to make the priestly garments. When completed it was a magnificent sight because of the sacrificial giving of the people of God. In fact, they gave so much that we read the following:

> Then all the craftsmen who were doing all the work of the sanctuary came, each from the work he was doing, and they spoke to Moses, saying, "The people bring much more than enough for the service of the work which the LORD commanded us to do." So Moses gave a commandment, and they caused it to be pro-

claimed throughout the camp, saying, "Let neither man nor woman do any more work for the offering of the sanctuary." And the people were restrained from bringing, for the material they had was sufficient for all the work to be done—indeed too much.[19]

Let's follow the example of the Children of Israel and the example of the Macedonians. They willingly gave to be partners in God's work. May we become *Grace Givers* like the Macedonians. Before you pull out your checkbook, there is one more principle of *Grace Giving* we can learn from the Macedonians.

They Gave With The Right Priority

One final principle that we need to learn from the Macedonian believers relates to their priorities in *grace giving*. Notice that the priority gift was **not** their money. The priority gift was to give their own *lives first*. God is more concerned about you than about your money. The beginning place of *grace giving* is to "*give yourself first*."

The second thing we should note about their priorities in giving is to whom they gave themselves. First, they gave themselves *to the Lord*. He is number one. Before we give ourselves to family, the church, or a ministry we must

---

19 Exodus 36:4-7

first give ourselves to God. *Grace giving* is about realizing that we belong to God. When we fully give ourselves to God, then He already has all our resources. When we give ourselves to God, He has the right to lead us to give ourselves and our resources to others.

Only after the Macedonians gave themselves to God could they give themselves to Paul. Having done this they willingly gave in such a way that they were partners in His ministry to the Judean believers. We give ourselves to God, then as He leads, we give ourselves to a ministry. When we do this, our resources will follow.

Several years back, I attended the State Convention meetings of the Southern Baptist Conservatives of Virginia. During one of the sessions, I was to speak about their partnership with the New Hampshire Baptist Association. As another speaker introduced me, he had a graphic placed on the screen behind me that showed a person standing inside an offering plate. The theme of the session was printed under the graphic. "Step into the plate." This is a vivid picture of the example of the Macedonians. They gave themselves first and then they gave their resources even going beyond their ability, trusting God to provide for their own needs. If you want to be a *grace giving partner,* you must first step into the plate, giving yourself to the Lord and then to the ministry He is leading you to support.

THE EXAMPLE OF THE MESSIAH

I speak not by commandment, but I am testing the sincerity of your love by the diligence of others. For you know the grace of our Lord Jesus Christ, that though He was rich, yet for your sakes He became poor, that you through His poverty might become rich. And in this I give advice: It is to your advantage not only to be doing what you began and were desiring to do a year ago; but now you also must complete the doing of it; that as there was a readiness to desire it, so there also may be a completion out of what you have. For if there is first a willing mind, it is accepted according to what one has, and not according to what he does not have. For I do not mean that others should be eased and you burdened; but by an equality, that now at this time your abundance may supply their lack, that their abundance also may supply your lack— that there may be equality. As it is written, "He who gathered much had nothing left over, and he who gathered little had no lack.[20]

In this paragraph the Apostle Paul continues to teach the Corinthians key principles of *Grace Giving*. He does this both by instruction as well as by example.

---

20 2 Corinthians 8:8–15

The example he uses must, without a doubt, be understood as the greatest example of giving the world has ever known. In verse 9 he says, **"For you know the grace of our Lord Jesus Christ, that though He was rich, yet for your sakes He became poor, that you through His poverty might become rich."**[21] Jesus the Messiah is the greatest example of *Grace Giving* we could consider. Bringing together the example of Jesus in verse nine, with the instructions to the Corinthians in verses eight and ten through fifteen, let me point out three specific principles of *Grace Giving* that Paul instructed the Corinthians to follow. *The Messiah Gave in Sincerity. The Messiah Gave Completely. The Messiah Gave Willingly.* Let's consider Jesus' example and follow it.

The Messiah Gave in Sincerity

Paul begins this paragraph by telling the Corinthians that he was not commanding them to give. His desire was not to demand, nor manipulate them into giving. We find here a stark contrast to the way some view giving today. Over the years of my involvement in ministry it has amazed me at how many people give out of guilt. One particular man told me several years ago that he just did not "feel right" about going to church unless he put money in the offering plate. Upon further examination it

---

21   2 Corinthians 8:9

became clear he was under compulsion to give each time he attended church. When he did attend, he gave out of a sense of duty. Yet Paul says that he does not want them to give simply based on a commandment. He had a higher purpose in mind.

Notice he says that he is asking them to give as a test of the "sincerity of (their) love." Paul wanted the Corinthians to give out of a sincere heart of love. He wanted them to give because they wanted to give. He wanted them to give because they were so overwhelmed with the *grace giving* of Jesus that they could not help but want to give as a reflection of His love.

This is exactly how Jesus gave. He gave not because He had to give. He gave because He loves us with an everlasting love. He gave because He wanted to give. He gave in complete sincerity. The Bible teaches us that when He was on the cross, He could have called 10,000 angels to end the injustice of His crucifixion. Yet because of His great love for us He allowed Himself to suffer and die for you and me. As Paul said in verse nine, **"though He was rich, yet for your sakes He became poor."**[22] Though He did not deserve death, He chose to die out of a heart of sincere love.

The key principle here is that *Grace Giving* follows the example of the Messiah and gives from a heart of love. In 1 Corinthians chapter thirteen, referred to by many as *The Love Chapter*, the Apostle Paul helps us understand

---

22 Ibid

the importance of giving from a heart of sincere love. **"And though I bestow all my goods to feed the poor, and though I give my body to be burned, but have not love, it profits me nothing."**[23] Paul writes that even if we were to give all we have, if it is not given out of a heart of sincere love we have missed the mark. Jesus gave in sincerity and so must we.

The Messiah Gave Completely

In verses ten and eleven Paul reminds the Corinthians of their past commitment to give. A year earlier they had desired to give and even began the process of planning to give. They may have even begun to receive offerings. An entire year has passed, and the Corinthians wavered in their commitment. Therefore, Paul tells them that they need to follow through with what they committed to do a year earlier.

Paul is concerned that the believers in Corinth return to their commitment the previous year. He wants them to bring the offering to completion. Twice in verse eleven he tells them to complete what they started. The Greek word used here is *epiteleo*. The word means to *perform to the finish, to bring to an end, to accomplish, to complete the task*. Both times Paul writes this in verse eleven, the Apostle uses the aorist tense in Greek. By doing this

---

23 1 Corinthians 13:3

he further emphasized a specific point in time when the task should be done.

Jesus completed His work on our behalf. Though He was tempted in the wilderness to take His eyes off the prize, He did not waver.[24] Though the weight was heavy in the Garden, He pressed on.[25] Though He was beaten, abandoned, mocked, spit upon, and crucified, He finished the task.[26] In fact, His own words on the cross give witness to what it means to give completely. As He hung there He cried out, *tetelestai* which is translated, *Paid in full* or *It is finished!*[27]

In Haggai we read of a group of believers who failed to finish the task God had set before them. After the 70 years of captivity these Jews returned to Jerusalem to rebuild the Temple of God. They were excited and rejoiced at the privilege. Before long however, they were distracted by lack of resources and concern for the restoration of their own houses. Through Haggai the Lord informed them that His hand of blessing had been withheld by their lack of completion. However, as the people returned to the right priorities and gave their time, talents, and resources to rebuild the Temple, the Lord promised renewed blessings upon them.[28]

---

24 Luke 4:1-13
25 Luke 22:39-46
26 Luke 22:47-23:56
27 John 19:30
28 Haggai 3

The one who practices *Grace Giving* not only gives in sincerity, but he/she gives completely. God is not only concerned in how we start but in how we finish. He wants us to give out of sincere love and to complete our commitments to give.

The Messiah Gave Willingly

Verse twelve begins with a conditional phrase, **"For if there is first a willing mind."**[29] We need to understand that God's first concern is your willingness. In fact, God is more concerned with the willingness of your mind and your heart than He is with the amount of your gift. God owns everything and He does not need your money. He will always provide for His work. The great thing is that many times He chooses to provide through you and me. He wants you to be willing to give.

The text teaches us that if we are willing to give, then it is acceptable to decide how much we will give based upon what we have. Though the Macedonians gave beyond their ability, Paul says if you have a willing mind than it is ok to give based on what you do have. Furthermore, he says it is not his desire that the Corinthians lack what they truly need. Rather, the intent is that everyone's needs be met. At this time, the Church at Corinth was doing well financially while those in Judea were in distress.

---

29 2 Corinthians 8:12

Therefore, he asks that they give to help their brothers and sisters in Christ.[30]

Without a doubt Jesus gave willingly. He said, **"No one takes my life but I lay it down."**[31] As noted earlier, the weight of the struggle was great. So great that the Bible tells us that when He was in the Garden of Gethsemane, He prayed three times concerning the trial of the cross. Yet, each time He willingly surrendered His will to the Father. He willingly laid down His life so that we might be forgiven and receive the gift of eternal life. He gave willingly.

Stop what you are doing for a moment and take the test of willingness. It is a simple test. All you have to do is ask yourself the following question, **"If God told me to sell everything I have and give the money to His work, would I do it?"** Now don't answer too quickly. Think about it. If you really knew the Lord was asking you to GIVE ALL, what would you do? He may never ask you to give all. However, He is concerned about your willingness. Do you give out of compulsion and duty, or do you give willingly?

Jesus is the greatest example of *Grace Giving*. He gave sincerely. He gave completely. He gave willingly. Let's follow His example.

---

30 2 Corinthians 8:13–15
31 John 10:18

THE EXHORTATIONS OF THE MISSIONARY

But this I say: He who sows sparingly will also reap sparingly, and he who sows bountifully will also reap bountifully. So let each one give as he purposes in his heart, not grudgingly or of necessity; for God loves a cheerful giver. And God is able to make all grace abound toward you, that you, always having all sufficiency in all things, may have an abundance for every good work. As it is written: "He has dispersed abroad, He has given to the poor; His righteousness endures forever." Now may He who supplies seed to the sower, and bread for food, supply and multiply the seed you have sown and increase the fruits of your righteousness, while you are enriched in everything for all liberality, which causes thanksgiving through us to God. For the administration of this service not only supplies the needs of the saints, but also is abounding through many thanksgivings to God, while, through the proof of this ministry, they glorify God for the obedience of your confession to the gospel of Christ, and for your liberal sharing with them and all men, and by their prayer for you, who long for you because of the exceeding grace of God in you. Thanks be to God for His indescribable gift![32]

---

32 2 Corinthians 9:6-15

Apart from Jesus Himself, Paul must be the greatest missionary of all church history. The Lord used him to reach thousands of individuals with the Gospel of Christ. In addition, Paul's missionary work was extended through those he mentored like Timothy, Luke, Titus, and many others. His influence continued to spread even after his death through the writing of thirteen New Testament Epistles.

When a church would receive a letter from the Apostle Paul, everyone was anxious to hear what he had to say. Paul's love for the Lord and for His people could not be denied. Over and over again he laid his life on the line for the opportunity to minister the Word to God's people and to lead the lost to faith in Christ. When Paul gave instructions, the early church paid attention.

Having laid before the Corinthians the *Example of The Macedonians* and the *Example of the Messiah*, Paul now turns his attention to a personal exhortation concerning this concept of *Grace Giving*. In the above paragraph the Apostle Paul reveals three exhortations that will lead the readers to truly become *Grace Givers*. First, he tells the Corinthian believers that to be a *Grace Giver* one must give generously. Second, he explains that *Grace Givers* must give cheerfully. Third, Paul conveys the fact that *Grace Givers* can give expectantly.

Grace Givers Give Generously

Paul begins the paragraph by focusing attention on the law of sowing and reaping. Of course, the idea of sowing and reaping is found throughout Scripture. In fact, Paul even reminded the Galatians that **"whatever a man sows that shall he also reap."**[33] We cannot sow apple seeds and expect to get oranges. Neither can we sow one apple seed and expect a grove to simply spring forth from that one seed without further sowing. Therefore, we should sow in accordance with the harvest we are looking to receive.

In verse six Paul takes the concept of sowing and reaping and applies it directly to *Grace Giving*. He does so by first pointing out that **"he who sows sparingly shall also reap sparingly."**[34] He wanted the Corinthians to understand that they could not expect to reap a liberal harvest if they were unwilling to sow liberally. Though God always meets the needs of His children, if they gave sparingly, they would also reap sparingly.

In the later part of the verse Paul contrasts this first statement by noting, **"he who sows bountifully will also reap bountifully."**[35] If the believers at Corinth were to give generously, they would also receive generously. The law of sowing and reaping is the same today as it was in

33 Galatians 6:7

34 2 Corinthians 9:6

35 Ibid

the first century. If you and I sow generously we will also reap generously.

From time to time, I am asked about tithing. Some people want to know why they should tithe. Others want to know what the big deal is about 10%. I have met many people over the years who focus on the tithe because they want to know what the minimum requirements are for giving. I have actually had people tell me that they tithe to "keep God happy." In contrast, the *Grace Giver* wants to give generously out of a heart of gratitude and love for God. For the *Grace Giver* the tithe is simply the starting place of giving. As Jesus lives through the individual, the *Grace Giver* goes over and above the tithe. The *Grace Giver* gives generously knowing that he can never out give the Lord.

Grace Givers Give Cheerfully

In verse seven Paul records his second exhortation to the *Grace Giver*. Not only does a *Grace Giver* give generously, but he also gives cheerfully. In describing cheerful giving the Apostle begins by saying that each one should give, "**as he purposes in his heart**."[36] In other words, Paul was not going to tell individuals how much they should give. He did not set a dollar amount. He simply left it up to each person to determine within their own heart how

---

36 2 Corinthians 9:7

much he/she should give. As you consider how much you should give to your church on a regular basis, let me offer a few suggestions:

1. Ask the Lord to show you what He would have you give.
2. Consider how much He has given you.
3. If you are married, talk it over with your spouse and pray about it together.
4. Make sure that your gift is generous.
5. Give as you believe the Lord has led you to give.

These same principles can be applied not only to your regular giving but also to special offerings and other opportunities you have. As you determine before God the amount He is leading you to give, give as He leads.

After explaining that a person should give as they purpose in their heart, Paul writes about how we should **not** give. Once we know how much the Lord is leading us to give, and we decide to proceed, it is important that we keep the right attitude. In the middle of the verse Paul warns us about two attitudes that the *Grace Giver* must avoid.

He says we are not to give *grudgingly*. In Greek he writes, we are not to give *ek lupe*. The phrase means, *out of grief*. A person may seek God for how much he/she should give and then be surprised at His leading. The giver may then proceed with the gift but do so out of a heart of grief and sorrow. Paul says this is wrong. We must not give out of sorrow.

A story told of a faithful circuit riding preacher named Robert Sheffey illustrates this point well. Brother Sheffey was known all over the South in the late nineteenth century as an amazing man of God. He prayed, preached, and practiced the Word of God. Folks began to say, that when Sheffey prayed God always answered.

One day as he was returning home from a preaching tour, riding on his faithful horse and good companion, he came upon a poor family. Mom, Dad, and children packed what little they had on a wagon and wandered about the wilderness looking for work. Not long before Sheffey arrived on the scene, the poor family's horse simply fell over dead. They had nowhere to turn and no money to buy a new horse.

As Robert realized the seriousness of their plight, he sat down alongside the road to pray that the Lord would provide for this needy family. Before long he looked up towards heaven and was heard to say, "Lord, would you require so much?" The preacher arose, unsaddled his trusty friend, and hooked him up to the family's wagon. As they protested, he told them that there was no sense praying any longer since the Lord had already provided the family with a horse. It was his joy to be used to meet their need. He picked up his saddle and began walking towards home.[37]

---

37 "Robert Sheffey, A Saint in the Wilderness" Unusual

Robert Sheffey sought the Lord and was surprised by the Lord's leading. He loved his horse, but he loved the Lord even more. Thus, he gave generously and didn't look back. He did not give out of grief nor sorrow but simply out of a heart of obedient love. When the Lord shows us what to give, when we purpose in our hearts to give, let's not give out of a heart of grief but out of a heart of love.

Paul warns us of a second negative attitude that the *Grace Giver* must avoid. He writes that we should not give "out of necessity." The *Grace Giver* does not give because he has to give. The *Grace Giver* gives because he wants to give. We should not give simply because there is a need. We should not give because of what others will think if we don't give. We should not give to try to earn God's favor. Paul says clearly that the *Grace Giver* does not give simply out of a sense of duty.

In contrast to grief and necessity, the *Grace Giver* gives "cheerfully." Here we have the Greek word, *hilaros* from which we get our English word, *hilarious*. The word emphasizes two important concepts. The first concept is *joy*. *Grace Givers* give joyously. The second idea is that of *promptness*. The *Grace Giver* is ready to give as soon as the Lord opens the opportunity. God loves it when His children give joyously and promptly.

Several years ago, a new game show took our nation by storm. Millions of people tuned in each night

Films, Bob Jones University

to watch Regis give away generous amounts of money. Everywhere you went you could find people talking about "Who Wants To Be A Millionaire?" One of the things that caught my attention about the show was the excitement and joy with which Regis would give away the money. I remember thinking to myself; "I wonder if he would be that excited to give the money if it came from his own pocket." It is easy for us to rejoice even to the point of hilarious laughter when someone receives a large, unexpected gift. But do we give with that same enthusiasm? The *Grace Giver* gives *hilariously*, *joyously*, and *promptly*.

Grace Givers Give Expectantly

In verses eight through eleven Paul gives his third exhortation to the Corinthian believers. Not only are they to give generously, not only are they to give cheerfully; but they are also to give expectantly. The fact is that God's grace is always abounding. Paul says, no matter how much we give, we must not forget that **"God is able to make His grace abound."**[38] Mercy is not getting what we deserve, grace is getting what we do not deserve. God continually makes His Grace *perisseuo* or *increase* and *abound* toward His children. His grace does not stop. No matter how much we can give we cannot out give the Lord.

---

38 2 Corinthians 9:8

Notice the second phrase of verse eight, "**that you, always having all sufficiency in all things.**"[39] Not only does Paul write that God's grace will not quit but he also declares that God will be sure that we have, "all sufficiency." On another occasion the Apostle expressed the same concept to the Church at Philippi. He says, "**and my God shall supply all your needs according to His riches in glory, by Christ Jesus.**"[40] The fact is no matter how much the *Grace Giver* gives, God is always going to make certain that His children have all they need.

Paul further exhorts the Corinthians by giving further explanation in the final phrase of the verse. He says that the Lord will give to us to the point that we "**may have an abundance for every good work.**"[41] In other words, as the *Grace Giver* gives the Lord will not only supply him enough for his own needs but enough that He will be able to give again. Notice how this theme is continued in verses nine through eleven.

As it is written: "He has dispersed abroad, He has given to the poor; His righteousness endures forever." Now may He who supplies seed to the sower, and bread for food, supply and multiply the seed you have sown and increase

---

39 Ibid

40 Philippians 4:19

41 2 Corinthians 9:8

the fruits of your righteousness, while you are enriched in everything for all liberality, which causes thanksgiving through us to God.[42]

Paul quotes from Psalm 112:9, thus supporting the concept that God gives to His children. He is righteous and thus will be faithful to fulfill His promise of provision. In verse ten Paul continues the theme by stating that He will **"provide seed to the sower."** Having begun this paragraph by encouraging the readers to sow generously, the Apostle now teaches us that as we give, God will supply additional seed to sow again so that our fruit may increase while at the same time providing us with **"bread for food."**

Finally, notice verse eleven. Here Paul tells us that we will be **"enriched for all liberality."** Thus, restating this important concept once again. As the *Grace Giver* gives, God will provide for the giver to the point that he will be able to continue to give and to give liberally. Paul wanted his readers to understand that when the *Grace Giver* gives generously and cheerfully, he can also give expectantly. Because God will not be out given. As we give God's way, He graciously gives to us. We can never out give the Lord. Almost 50 years ago, I heard a song that captures the essence of this principle. Consider the following words:

---

42 2 Corinthians 9:9–11

I'm going to live the way He wants me to live,
I'm going to give the way He wants me to give.
I'm going to love, love, till there's just no more
love, Cause I could never, no never, out love the
Lord, I could never, no never, out give the Lord.[43]

The fact is that the more we give, the more we love,
the more we learn that we could never out give, nor out
love the Lord. As we give generously and cheerfully we can
give expectantly. God will supply all your needs...and more!

CONCLUSION

Remember my story about our first church planting expe-
rience? In an attempt to not be an offense, I robbed God's
people by not teaching them the importance of *Grace Giving*. In fact, I robbed them of one form of Worship. The
act of *Grace Giving* is truly an avenue of worship directed
towards God. When we learn to give out of a heart of love
and gratitude, we are praising God for His grace that He
has bestowed on us. We then learn to know Him better
as we watch Him provide for our every need even to the
degree that we are empowered to give again. I often won-

---

43 "I Could Never Out Love The Lord" Special Music
performed by the Vandenberg Family at Park Hill Christian
Academy Pueblo, CO 1978

der if those new believers from Dallas, TX have ever had someone teach them this important concept. Though I cannot go back and change my mistakes of the past, I can do different today. Therefore, I teach God's people the importance of worshiping the Lord through *Grace Giving*.

Let me ask you. When the offering plate comes by you, how do you give? Do you give out of a sense of duty? Do you tithe because you feel like you must? Or do you follow the **Example of the Macedonians**? Do you follow the **Example of Jesus**? Do you follow the **Exhortations of the Missionary**?

Next time the offering plate comes by try approaching your giving the way my friend, Daniel Akin encouraged me to do many years ago. Close your eyes for just a minute and picture Jesus. There He is, hanging on the cross, giving His all for you. Then simply ask the Lord, "Jesus, in light of Your grace, how much do You want me to give?" Open your eyes and give generously, cheerfully, and expectantly.